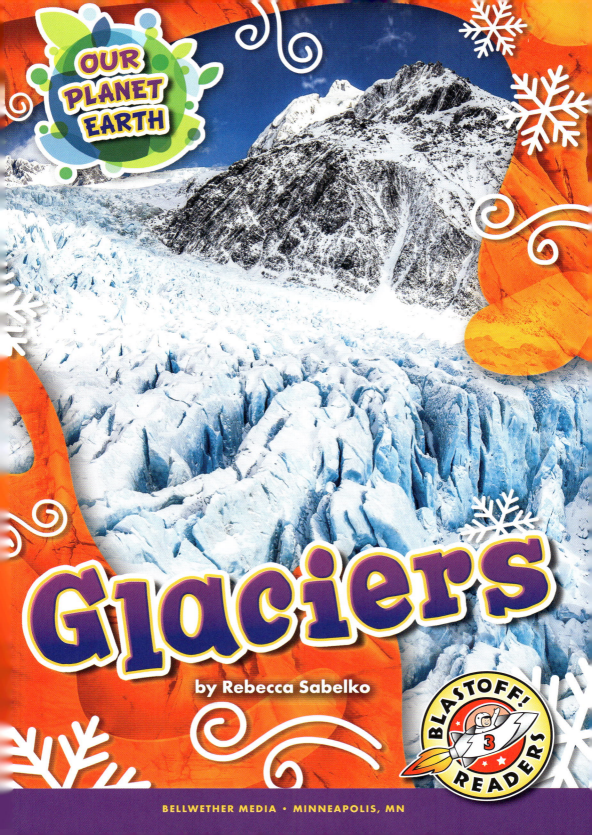

OUR PLANET EARTH

Glaciers

by Rebecca Sabelko

BELLWETHER MEDIA • MINNEAPOLIS, MN

BLASTOFF! READERS

3

Blastoff! Readers are carefully developed by literacy experts to build reading stamina and move students toward fluency by combining standards-based content with developmentally appropriate text.

Level 1 provides the most support through repetition of high-frequency words, light text, predictable sentence patterns, and strong visual support.

Level 2 offers early readers a bit more challenge through varied sentences, increased text load, and text-supportive special features.

Level 3 advances early-fluent readers toward fluency through increased text load, less reliance on photos, advancing concepts, longer sentences, and more complex special features.

★ **Blastoff! Universe**

Reading Level

Grade **K**

Grades **1–3**

Grade **4**

This edition first published in 2022 by Bellwether Media, Inc.

No part of this publication may be reproduced in whole or in part without written permission of the publisher. For information regarding permission, write to Bellwether Media, Inc., Attention: Permissions Department, 6012 Blue Circle Drive, Minnetonka, MN 55343.

Library of Congress Cataloging-in-Publication Data

LC record for Glaciers available at: https://lccn.loc.gov/2021045049

Editor: Kieran Downs   Designer: Laura Sowers

Printed in the United States of America, North Mankato, MN.

Table of Contents

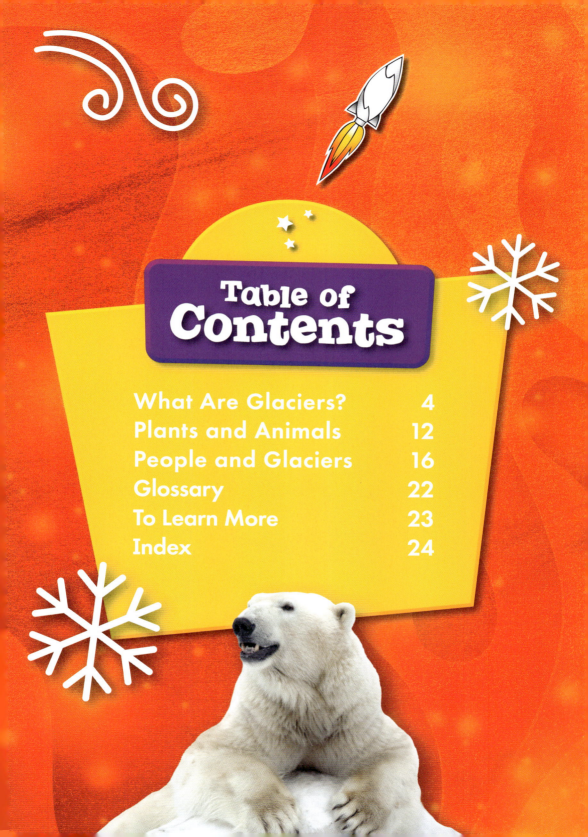

What Are Glaciers?

Glaciers are huge sheets of ice. They move slowly over land. Some glaciers may be around one million years old!

Glaciers cover around one-tenth of Earth's land. They hold well over half of Earth's freshwater!

Glaciers form where more snow falls than melts. Snow builds up and **compresses**. It becomes ice.

Glacier Formation

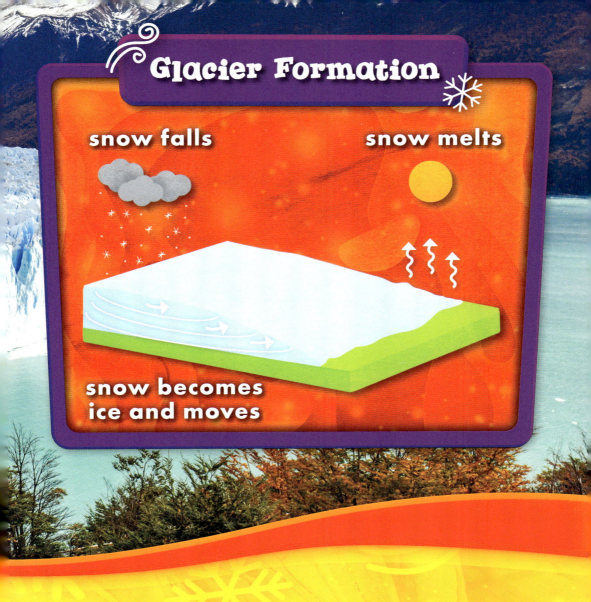

snow falls

snow melts

snow becomes
ice and moves

Gravity and the weight of the ice cause glaciers to move.

alpine glacier

moraine

Alpine glaciers move down mountains. They push rocks and dirt. This forms valleys and **moraines**.

Continental glaciers spread over large areas. The largest cover parts of Greenland and Antarctica.

Bering Glacier

Alaska

Bering Glacier

Famous For

- North America's largest and longest glacier

Size

- Area of more than 1,900 square miles (4,921 square kilometers)
- Around 125 miles (201 kilometers) long

Crevasses are cracks that run deep into glaciers. They form when parts of glaciers move at different speeds.

Lambert Glacier

Antarctica

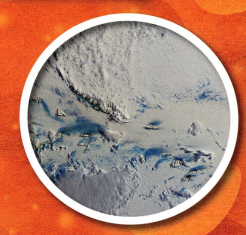

☐ = Lambert Glacier

Famous For

- World's largest glacier
- One of the world's fastest moving glaciers

Size

- More than 60 miles (97 kilometers) wide
- Around 270 miles (435 kilometers) long

moulin

Moulins form as water falls through crevasses. These holes go all the way to the ground.

Plants and Animals

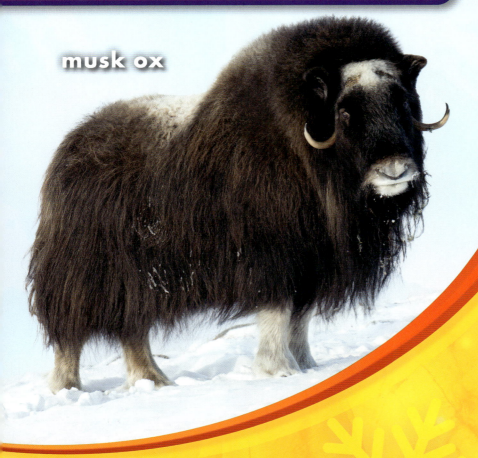

musk ox

Many plants and animals
are found on glaciers.
Finches build nests on ice.

Wolverines store food in glaciers.
Musk oxen travel across the ice.
They watch for hungry polar bears.

Glacier Animals

white-winged diuca-finch

polar bear

wolverine

elk

Ice worms survive in ice cracks. They wiggle to the surface each night to eat **algae**.

ice worm

← algae

glacier mouse

Balls of moss roll across some glaciers. Scientists often call them glacier mice!

People and Glaciers

Meltwater from glaciers is important to people. It is used for drinking and farming. People build **dams** to use meltwater for power.

Glaciers are popular places to visit, too. People hike on glaciers. They enjoy their beauty.

dam

17

Climate change is causing glaciers to melt faster than usual. The melting releases gases that warm Earth.

Meltwater flows into oceans. This causes sea levels to rise. It also changes ocean **habitats**.

How People Affect Glaciers

- Climate change causes glaciers to melt faster than usual

- Melting releases gases that warm Earth

- Melting causes sea levels to rise and changes ocean habitats

People must slow climate change to save glaciers. They can travel less or buy fewer products. They can make less waste.

People and businesses can use less **energy**. Glaciers will stay frozen if people work together!

Glossary

algae—plants and plantlike living things; most kinds of algae grow in water.

alpine glaciers—glaciers that move down mountains

climate change—a human-caused change in Earth's weather due to warming temperatures

compresses—presses or squeezes together

continental glaciers—glaciers that begin from their center and spread over a large area of land

crevasses—deep, narrow openings or cracks in glaciers

dams—structures built by people to stop water from flowing

energy—the power to move and do things

gravity—the force that pulls objects toward one another

habitats—areas with certain types of plants, animals, and weather

meltwater—water formed by the melting of snow and ice

moraines—piles of earth and stone left by glaciers

moulins—holes in glaciers that form from meltwater on the surface dripping into crevasses

To Learn More

AT THE LIBRARY

Fowler, Susi Gregg. *Who Lives Near a Glacier?* Seattle, Wash.: Sasquatch Books, 2022.

Gardner, Jane P. *How Glaciers Shaped Earth.* Minneapolis, Minn.: Jump!, 2021.

Kenney, Karen Latchana. *Oceans.* Minneapolis, Minn.: Bellwether Media, 2022.

ON THE WEB

FACTSURFER

Factsurfer.com gives you a safe, fun way to find more information.

1. Go to www.factsurfer.com.

2. Enter "glaciers" into the search box and click 🔍.

3. Select your book cover to see a list of related content.

Index

The images in this book are reproduced through the courtesy of: Matt Makes Photos, front cover; Zhiltsov Alexandr, p. 3; Cristian E Rodriguez, pp. 4-5; Oleg Senkov, p. 5; saiko3p, pp. 6-7; Wildnerdpix, p. 8; Design Pics Inc / Alamy Stock Photo, pp. 8-9, 9; RGB Ventures / Super Stock / Alamy Stock Photo, p. 10; DCrane, pp. 10-11; Giedriius, p. 12; Jonathan Chancasana, p. 13 (white-winged diuca-finch); FloridaStock, p. 13 (polar bear); Karel Bartik, p. 13 (wolverine); Michael Overstreet, p. 13 (elk); Southwick3, p. 14; Dene' Miles, pp. 14-15; Michael Marquand / Alamy Stock Photo, p. 15; Swedishnomad.com - Alex W, p. 16; NicoElNino, pp. 16-17; MomentumStock, pp. 18-19; R.M. Nunes, pp. 20-21; Marti Bug Catcher, p. 23.